Raising the Family without Taking a Hit

Raising the Family
Without Taking a Hit

How to Make Use of Your Cash Assets to Generate High
Rates of Interest While Perpetuating the Principal

Pierre Mouchette

Raising the Family Without Taking a Hit

© 2016 by Real Property Experts LLC

Published by Real Property Experts LLC

All rights reserved. No part of this publication may be reproduced or transmitted in any form or by any means, electronic or mechanical, including photocopying, recording, or any information storage and retrieval system, except as permitted under Section 107 or 108 of the 1976 United States Copyright Act, without the prior permission of the publisher.

ISBN 10: 1537526723
ISBN 13: 9781537526720

Printed in the United States

This publication is designed to provide accurate and authoritative information with regard to the subject matter covered. It is sold with the understanding that the publisher is not engaged in rendering legal, accounting, or other professional advice. If legal advice or other expert assistance is required, the services of a competent professional person should be sought (from a *Declaration of Principles* jointly adopted by a Committee of the American Bar Association and a Committee of Publishers and Associations).

Library of Congress Control Number: 2016914961

CreateSpace Independent Publishing Platform, North Charleston, SC

Raising the Family Without Taking a Hit

This book is dedicated to the
Mouchette family members.

I would also like to express a special thank-you to
Tomasa, my wife,
for her contribution in helping to edit the manuscript.
She spent many evenings and weekends
reading every word of each and every page.
I appreciate your observations,
thoughts, and, above all, patience and time.

Raising the Family Without Taking a Hit

Table of Contents

SECTION 1   General Information .... - 9 -
    1.0   Introduction .... - 9 -
    1.1   What Is a Tax Lien Investor? .... - 9 -
    1.2   Operating Your Investment Business .... - 9 -
    1.3   Investor Policy .... - 10 -
    1.4   Investment Operations Manual .... - 10 -
        Sample: Investment Operations Manual (IOM) .... - 11 -
SECTION 2   Personal Loans .... - 14 -
    2.0   Introduction .... - 14 -
    2.1   Policy .... - 14 -
    2.2   Personal Loan Amount .... - 14 -
    2.3   The Software .... - 15 -
    2.4   The Penalty .... - 15 -
    2.5   The Note .... - 15 -
        Sample: Promissory Note .... - 16 -
SECTION 3   Loan Servicing .... - 17 -
    3.0   Introduction .... - 17 -
    3.1   The Program .... - 17 -
    3.2   Service Costs .... - 19 -
SECTION 4   Tax Lien Certificates .... - 20 -
    4.0   Introduction .... - 20 -
    4.1   Tax Lien Certificates .... - 22 -
    4.2   Due Diligence .... - 22 -
    4.3   Peculiarities in Tax Liens Awarding .... - 24 -
    4.4   The Tax Sale .... - 25 -

4.5	Protect Your Investment	- 26 -
4.6	Bidding Systems	- 27 -
4.7	Assigning Tax Liens	- 28 -
4.8	Getting Paid	- 29 -
4.9	Additional Benefits	- 29 -
4.10	Conclusion	- 29 -
4.11	Tax Lien Software	- 29 -
4.12	Example of a Tax Lien Investment Account	- 30 -

SECTION 5   Cash Flow ....- 33 -

| 5.0 | Introduction | - 33 - |
| 5.1 | Basic Calculations | - 33 - |

SECTION 6   The Home Office ....- 35 -

6.0	According to the IRS	- 35 -
6.1	Home Setup	- 36 -
6.2	Internet	- 36 -

APPENDIX A ....- 37 -

APPENDIX B ....- 40 -

APPENDIX C ....- 43 -

APPENDIX D ....- 46 -

APPENDIX E ....- 50 -

PREFACE

The purpose of *Raising the Family without Taking a Hit* is to provide a clear and concise method from which the real estate investor can make use of his or her cash assets for himself or herself and family while continuing to maintain the asset's principal and have it earn interest at a higher rate than through the purchase of high-yield Certificates of Deposit.

This manual may contain general legal and accounting principles and is not meant to be a substitute for consulting an attorney and an accountant. It is to be used as a guide for obtaining the indicated use.

The book is written in an easy-to-read format for instant implementation.

Pierre Mouchette, author

Raising the Family Without Taking a Hit

Recycle, Recycle, Recycle!

To make family money (for portfolio)

To have family money (for family and portfolio)

To recycle family money (for legacy)

To retain family portfolio for recycling

Pierre Mouchette

SECTION 1   General Information

1.0   Introduction

There are many different types of investment vehicles that one can apply investment capital to beyond the traditional stocks, bonds, and certificates of deposit. For the purposes of this book, we will focus on tax lien certificates.

Children—you have them, nurture them, provide them with housing, and do your best to prepare them for their adult years. As time slips by, your children are now ready to leave home or go away to college. What do you do now? When the birds leave the nest, they must fly, or they will not survive. Hopefully, the foundation that you have instilled in them will give them the ability to make good life decisions.

Now the question comes up: Do you pay for their apartments, their college educations, and what other choices they may make? Where does it stop! It has often been said, "If you do not earn it, you do not appreciate it." Is this the answer!

Tax lien investments present a fantastic opportunity to help solve the question. Help them—the key word is "help"—but let them manage to do it on their own.

1.1   What Is a Tax Lien Investor?

A tax lien investor is a private investor that invests his or her own funds in delinquent taxes owed by individuals to the local government. Since the private investor does not deal with the public per se, he or she is not subjected to many of the social laws that encumber traditional investors.

1.2   Operating Your Investment Business

One of the first things that you must do is to open a small-business checking account and a money market account linked to each other. This account must be used specifically for this investment business.

1.3 Investor Policy

As a businessperson, you should have a standard operational policy by which you operate and run your business. The most successful investors run their businesses as businesses. Fortunately, the tax lien acquisition business is not a full-time business and can be run from your personal computer.

1.4 Investment Operations Manual

To start this investment business you should create an investment operation manual (IOM) containing guidelines for this asset. The IOM serves as a guide to effectively manage, monitor, and evaluate the acquisition of tax lien certificates. The IOM will help:

- to ensure compliance with fiduciary and prudent investor responsibilities and

- to set forth a structure for managing funds, including a spending rule, strategic asset allocation, and permissible ranges, that, when combined, are expected to produce an adequate level of return.

Sample: Investment Operations Manual (IOM)
___

Investment Operations Manual

The investment accounts' assets shall be commingled and broken down into two pools: short term and long term. The short-term pool (support) will provide cash for emergency funds, family loans, and tax lien reserves for subsequent taxes due focus on preservation and availability of cash. The long-term pool shall be well diversified by investing in tax lien certificates to satisfy the primary objective of preservation of capital with the secondary objective of maximizing the total returns on investment assets. The accounts assets, being commingled, will have the pools allocated by percentage.

The asset manager may also reposition a portion of assets held in the long-term investment pool to the short-term pool to cover anticipated short-term expenses.

At all times, the asset manager will keep appropriate records on the long-term pool's funds:

General

- purchase dates
- redemption dates
- registration deadlines
- foreclosure dates
- subsequent taxes due dates
- all other dates

Tax lien financial information

- cost of lien
- face value of lien
- subsequent costs incurred

- property values (assessed, improved, land, fair market)
- accrual basis and rate

The Asset Account

The asset's funds will be kept in a commercial bank account, this account being a small-business checking account linked to a money market account. This combination will maximize your savings while maintaining access to cash and earning interest on checking.

Money market account: This is where you keep the short-term funds. In maintaining more than the bank's minimum balance, you have no upkeep charges and receive the stated interest rate. An additional benefit is that you can transfer money to the checking account as warranted.

Business checking account: From this account, you purchase the tax lien certificates and pay for abstractors' services and other costs of doing business. As the liens are redeemed, the principal, interest, and other fees earned are deposited, thereby replenishing available funds for future tax lien acquisitions. Also, since the accounts are linked, funds are available for transfer as needed.

Rate of Return

The minimum rate of return is 8 percent. This is the amount equal to the expected rate of spending, expressed as a percentage. The actual rate of return on the portfolio for any given year will include dividends, interest, and realized and unrealized gains and losses. With experience, the asset manager will increase the rate of return.

Spending Rules

Spending rules provide a disciplined approach for determining how the funds are spent and for the distribution of funds for short- and long-term objectives.

Short-term spending:

> Having readily available cash for emergency funds, family loans, and tax lien reserves is of the utmost importance and the main reason for this asset account. The asset manager will determine the amount of money to make available for this account, depending on ongoing family needs and reserves for subsequent taxes due on purchased tax liens. Initially, the asset manager will use a percentage of the gross funds available for the investment business (i.e., emergency funds/family loans reserve 10 percent, tax lien reserve 5 percent).

Long-term spending:

> Long-term spending or the acquisition of tax liens will provide the investment account with ongoing funds for reinvestment and transfers to the money market account as needed. The asset manager will determine the amount of money to be retained in the account, for the purchase of tax lien certificates and maximizing the return on investment. Initially, the asset manager will use a percentage of the gross funds available for the investment business (i.e., 85 percent).

SECTION 2   Personal Loans

2.0   Introduction

As previously stated, there comes a time when children and family members need money. Sometimes just saying no can complicate family ties or providing the recipient with a loan will create other financial problems. The solution to this dilemma is to set a standard written policy for this situation.

2.1   Policy

As you know, personal lending to family members has been around since man first learned to count and have others in the clan. If you lend to a family member remember, **"Memories fade and disagreements do arise."** Protect yourself by creating and signing a document called a "promissory note" that lists the amount, interest charged, and repayment schedule.

2.2   Personal Loan Amount

A workable solution would be:

- All personal loans when made are for a term of no more than twenty-four months and for a minimum of $2,000 and a maximum amount of $9,000. If the loan amount is for more than $9,000, have a loan servicing company handle the loan for you. The borrower can pay the setup and handling fees (build it into the note).

- The interest rate should be as stated on bankrate.com for your state and county.

    If the IRS learns that you have given an interest-free loan, it can impute interest on the loan to you!

2.3 The Software

TimeValue Software (TValue Amortization Software) will provide you with amortizing loans and time value of money calculations. These schedules print in seconds.

2.4 The Penalty

Make it known to the borrower (family member) that the loan has to be repaid as indicated on the loan schedule. Failure to comply with payments on the agreed schedule will cancel any future monies to them! If you use a "loan servicing company," it will handle problems like any other major lender.

2.5 The Note

Use the following standard note for transactions under $9,000. If the loan is for more than $9,000, have your attorney draw up the loan document and use a loan servicing company.

Sample: Promissory Note
___

PROMISSORY NOTE

I_____ (individually) or we_____, (jointly and severally), promise to pay to_____, lender, the principal amount of _____ (written in both figures and in words) plus interest.

Interest shall be charged at the rate of _____% (specify payment period or per year). Interest shall accrue from the date this note is signed and money loaned until the date the note is paid off in full.

The note shall be paid in _____ (number) installments of $_____ (dollar amount), in numerals and words) beginning on _____ (date due) and on the _____ day of each month thereafter until the principal and interest are paid in full.

Each payment shall first be applied to unpaid accrued interest, and the remainder will be applied to the remaining balance of principal.

If the lender does not receive any payment due under this note within FIVE days of its due date, the entire note of unpaid principal and accrued but unpaid interest shall become immediately due and payable at the option of the lender without the need of any additional notice to the borrowers.

If the lender prevails in a lawsuit to collect this note, I/we agree to pay the lender's court costs and attorney's fees in any amount the court finds reasonable.

Should the borrower pay off the entire loan prior to its due date, the interest will be recalculated so that there is no prepayment penalty.

_____   _____
Borrower Signature   Lender Signature
_____   _____
Print Name   Date   Print Name   Date

Address   Address

City, State, Zip   City, State, Zip

Telephone Number   Telephone Number

SECTION 3   Loan Servicing

3.0   Introduction

Many companies offer streamlined loan servicing solutions specifically designed for the private investor. These programs provide the investor with a customized loan servicing function designed as an extension of their existing business operations. Through the implementation of the programs, the investor will maximize revenue, optimize management controls, and provide exceptional customer service.

3.1   The Program

The standard program usually consists of payment processing, basic collections, and default servicing:

A. Payment processing

- borrower welcome letter
- borrower monthly statement with payment coupon and return envelope
- lender welcome letter
- lender monthly statement of all accounts
- same-day payment posting
- daily disbursement of funds by automated clearing house (ACH) into lender's account
- optional escrow/impound service for insurance and taxes
- payoff demands
- rush demands
- disbursements and draws

- releases and reconveyances
- IRS 1098 and 1099-INT reporting
- online secure account access twenty-four seven for investor/lender
- downloadable reports for investor/lender

B. Basic collection

- late notice sent
- final notice sent
- borrower inquiry calls handled
- act as intermediary between borrower and investor / lender
- notify investor/lender of borrower's need for refinance or modification

C. Default servicing

- specific thirty-day Notice of Intent letters
- foreclosure process started immediately upon written request by investor/lender
- national foreclosure processing or coordination
- legal services coordination including bankruptcy relief and eviction
- Real Estate Owned (REO) management and property sale availability

3.2   Service Costs

The following are basic (guide) service costs:

Loan setup fee	$25 (one time per loan)
Payment processing	$15 per month
HELOC (home equity line of credit) and/or ARM (adjustable rate mortgage)	$5 per month
Escrow impounds	$25 per month

SECTION 4   Tax Lien Certificates

4.0   Introduction

Local governments provide services such as police protection, public schooling, medical services, road maintenance, and much more. The inability to collect real estate property taxes curtails the services that they provide. Every state and territory in the United States has a process in place to collect delinquent taxes. This process occurs at the last juncture of the tax-collection process, and it allows ordinary individuals (investors) the right to purchase tax lien certificates.

A real estate tax lien is an involuntary statutory lien, created by statute without any action by the property owner. There are two types of real estate taxes: a general real estate tax (also called ad valorem taxes) and special assessment or improvement taxes. Both are levied against specific parcels of property and automatically become liens on those properties.

A. At auction, the tax lien is sold with the following charges:

- delinquent property taxes
- interest charges
- penalty charges
- legal costs
- administrative charges and fees

B. Real estate tax liens are superior to judgment liens, mortgage liens, trust deeds, and other private liens. **IRS liens cannot be wiped clean.**

We repeat: IRS liens cannot be wiped clean.

The property tax lien is a priority lien position. The priority position of the property tax lien is not subordinated (or diminished) because a private party (investor) now holds the lien. This helps the investor because the foreclosure of your first-position tax lien will clear almost all other liens from the title. Foreclosure not only places full property ownership in the hands of the investor but also purges the land title of other subordinate liens and debts. The result is a property interest that is generally free and clear of other obligations on the title.

Tax liens

A. When a property owner (taxpayer) does not pay his or her property taxes, an encumbrance or property lien called a tax lien is placed on the property. The tax lien does not grant full ownership rights to the property, but it does provide the investor with the following rights:

- the right of a super priority lien holder (The investor has no property owner liability or maintenance responsibility until the property is foreclosed upon.)

- the right to receive interest penalty charges if the delinquent property owner pays off the lien (The taxing body will handle the enforcement of the lien until it is foreclosed upon. Some states will even handle the foreclosure process for you. As the investor, you do not have any contact with the delinquent taxpayer. In the redemption scenario, the tax office will handle the collection of redemption money plus interest.)

- the right to privately acquire the taxes without competition if the property owner defaults on the following year's taxes.

- the right to foreclose the tax lien (this is called a lien conversion) and take title to the property if the lien is not paid before the redemption period has expired.

B. Generally, the delinquent taxpayer can redeem the property any time before the tax sale. The taxpayer exercises his or her "equitable right of redemption" by paying delinquent taxes plus interest and charges (any court costs or attorney's fees).

C. A "certificate of sale" is given to the successful bidder when the investor purchases the delinquent tax amount.

4.1   Tax Lien Certificates

Tax lien certificates are rarely foreclosed on. (The mortgage companies will pay off delinquent taxes rather than lose the principal.) Because of this, **tax liens are a good stream of income.**

4.2   Due Diligence

Due diligence is checking out all the available details on a property. The most direct way is to go to the town hall (hall of records, office of the prothonotary are all the same place). Generally, due diligence for tax-delinquent properties consists of the following:

A. Assessor's office: The tax assessor maintains a list of taxable properties in the municipality. This Grand List contains an estimate of the value of all properties.

- Field card: A document containing information on a property such as the land size, its improvements, and the methodology of the assessment. The card also contains the volume and page that the transaction is recorded in.

B. Town clerk's office: The town clerk is responsible for maintaining all public records, which include deeds, mortgages, notes, leases, mechanics' liens, and attachments. Each record is stamped with the date, time, and signature acknowledging its official receipt and entry of the document into the public record.
- Daybook: Because of the lapse of time in recording a document and the town's clerk indexing it in the Grantor/Grantee lists, the records are catalogued in a

daybook. Always refer to the daybook before going to the Grantor/Grantee lists.

- Grantor/Grantee lists: The town clerk maintains lists separate from all other recorded documents containing information on local real estate transactions indexed under the names of the Grantors and Grantees. These lists are a chronological compilation of all types of documents received for recording and make it easy to trace a specific parcel's chain of title.

C. Physical inspection: Go to the property and verify that it has everything that the field card claims. If the card states that there is a dwelling and garage, *verify!* You do not want to purchase a tax lien certificate on a burned-out building, vacant land or any other type of property with no redeemable value.

D. Internet: Use the Internet by inserting the complete address. If you are lucky, you will be able to see a picture of the property plus other relevant information.

E. Abstractors: If the property is located too far for you to accomplish A–C, employ the services of an abstractor. An abstractor can:

- provide lot, parcel, and property characteristics (zoning, flood, and easement maps);

- current owner(s) of title and tax mailing address;

- chain of title and transfers with full sale history;

- provide copies of records and deeds (federal, state, and local tax liens, bankruptcies, and judgments);

- order mortgage payoffs;

- provide copies of delinquent tax records and amounts;

- notice of default, auction, REO;

- foreclosure status reports;
- property asset and title search by name;
- Multiple Listing Service (MLS) photos available with reports; and
- property valuation reports for comparable MLS and FSBO (for sale by owner) sales.

Abstract companies offer different levels of service and have different prices accordingly. You must decide how much information you need to make an informed decision. We have provided a list of abstractors in the appendix. Although this list is nowhere complete, you can use it as a starting point.

4.3 Peculiarities in Tax Liens Awarding

Some states use a random selection or round robin process to award the tax lien certificates. The downfall to this selection process is that you cannot do your due diligence on all of the properties; you can only accept or decline the offering.

Two other states to be aware of are:

- The Commonwealth of Kentucky accepts bids for the amount due and costs by mail, e-mail, fax, and in person, and the first bid received is awarded the tax lien. The bidder must be present at the sale to be awarded the tax lien certificate.
- Alaska does not offer tax liens or tax deeds. After the one-year redemption period, the taxing municipalities take ownership of the property and sell the property at fair market value to the public. Alaska's Department of Natural Resources also sells parcels separately from the local jurisdictions through OTC (over the counter) sales.

4.4   The Tax Sale

There are three types of tax sales: attended, mail, and online. Due diligence is required as each state, county, or municipality may have additional or more stringent rules and regulations.

Attended: The individual bidding at the auction must be authorized to purchase property on behalf of the entity to be listed on the tax deed and provide the required corporate or power of attorney documentation. The successful bidder must produce valid photo identification (driver's license, passport) and provide a telephone number. Upon successful completion of each bid, the successful bidder is required to have a nonrefundable cashier's check or money order deposit. A registration form must be completed at that time. The opening bid is the amount owed in back taxes, interest, and fees. The bid amount may not include all property taxes (previous years).

- The deposit amount varies by state and location.
- All bids are final at the end of the auction or during breaks.
- Settlement time varies by state and location.

Mail: Deliver your proposal with a cover letter signed by the purchaser, which includes an overview of the proposal as well as name, title, and the telephone number of the contact person. The letter should also include a statement accepting all terms and conditions contained in the request for proposal and a bank check in the required amount. The proposal should include at a minimum:

- transmittal
- title page

Online: To participate in the sale, a bidder must register and fill out a W-9 form with the revenue-collecting authority via its website. Registered bidders must provide a Federal Taxpayer Identification number or Social Security number. A bidder number is assigned for identification purposes during the sale. Bidders are usually required to make a deposit via ACH debit on the authority's website for 10 percent of the amount they intend to purchase. The deposit can be increased at any time prior to close of the auction.

- Successful bidders receive an email invoice indicating the total amount due. Failure to pay for all certificates at the due date will result in the loss of the deposit and forfeiture of all the certificates. The certificates will be sold at a later date.

- Refunds for unused portions of the deposit will be issued by check (in a few weeks) after the conclusion of the tax certificate sale.

4.5   Protect Your Investment
The following actions or nonactions will affect your investment:

- Many states require further actions be taken after being awarded the tax lien certificate to protect the lienholder's rights, generally within a certain time.

- Tax liens are not liquid and cannot be "cashed in." Tax liens are held until they are repaid or assigned to another person or until the lienholder acts to foreclose.

The following, though not inclusive, are some of the no cost-recoverable circumstances that could affect the amount of interest you earn on your investment and/or the amount you invest:

- owner files bankruptcy (interest could be reduced and/or trustee will send you $xx per month, etc.)

- Department of Revenue correction on the taxes

- court orders the omitting of taxes

- assessed value of the property may be in error and not subject to retroactive correction when the problem is discovered

- parcel may have had an assessed structure or wood-frame home that is subsequently burned down or condemned
- parcel may have had a mobile home on it at the time of the tax certificate sale that has been removed or destroyed, leaving the property vacant

4.6 Bidding Systems

After you complete your due diligence, it is time to review the list of properties and start your preliminary selection of probable properties. This selection will rely heavily on what state the sale is in and whether it is a tax lien or a tax deed sale.

A. For each property bid, note the maximum that you are willing to pay for it. The six most common types of bidding systems are:

1. Bidding down the interest rate: Under this method, the stated rate of return offered by the government is the maximum rate of return allowed. The investor can bid a lower rate of return, with the investor seeking the lowest interest rate winning the bid. In the event, there are more than one "lowest bids," a random or rotational method is used to break the ties. If no one offers a rate below the statutory rate but several bidders have raised their cards, the official will sell the lien to one of the investors at par by picking the investor at random. This bidding method occurs in Arizona, Florida, and Illinois and in Nassau County, New York.

2. Bidding up the cost (premium or overbid): With this method, the investor willing to pay the highest "premium" above the lien is the winner. One of the following systems is employed:

    - The premium and the lien both receive the same interest rate or penalty.

- The premium and the lien both receive interest but at different rates.
- The lien amount receives interest, while the premium does not.
- The premium amount does receive interest, while the lien amount does not.
- The premium is lost (the investor does not receive his or her principal back on any premium paid).

3. Random selection: The tax collector or auctioneer randomly selects bidders, usually by bidder number, for each parcel as it is read out at the sale. If the bidder does not want the property, the tax collector or auctioneer moves on to the next bidder. Used in Wyoming and Oklahoma.

4. Round robin: The tax collector goes around the room, offering the next parcel on the list to the next bidder in line. A random selection of awarding tax lien certificates from the governing jurisdiction. The downfall to this selection process is that you cannot do your due diligence on the properties. Used in some counties in Colorado for liens under a certain amount (the amount differs by county).

5. Over the counter (OTC): The tax parcel is sold without going through a public auction. Most OTC parcels can be purchased on the telephone, online, or by mail.

6. Sealed-envelope bidding: You place your bid in a sealed envelope, and the highest bidder wins.

4.7 Assigning Tax Liens

Tax liens can be sold (transferred or assigned) to another investor by completing an endorsement form, having the paperwork notarized, and paying the applicable fees. The new owner must be a registered buyer, and have completed and filed form W-9, and provided a Federal Taxpayer Identification number or Social Security number.

Not all certificates are transferrable. An example is where a deed application has been submitted.

4.8 Getting Paid

There are two ways of realizing a return on your tax lien certificate investment:

- When the property owner finally pays the property tax bill (delinquent taxes, interest, and/or penalty), the taxing authority cuts a check to the investor for the initial principal (tax bill) and the interest or penalty return. Note: The property owner or mortgage company can pay the property lien.

- If the property owner does not pay off the lien, you can foreclose on the property at the end of the redemption period.

4.9 Additional Benefits

Travel and expenses incurred are part of your operational expenses.

4.10 Conclusion

Tax liens are a great investment since they are backed by real property and administered by the government. They provide great cash flow since they are being continuously redeemed.

4.11 Tax Lien Software

Purchasing tax liens can be intimidating due to massive amount of information that you must retain and keep catalogued in an easy-to-reach format. To accomplish this, Tax Lien Software (http://www.taxliensoftware.com) has created an easy-to-use software program. The program will help you:

- record tax lien certificate information
- maintain contact and vital information
- enter significant dates
- enter tax lien financial data

Additionally, the software lets you enter significant dates with pop-up reminders so that you will never miss an important date. All of this and the ability to print out various types of reports make this truly a worthwhile expenditure.

4.12 Example of a Tax Lien Investment Account

Purchasing tax liens is an investment and, like any investment, it must be executed in a diligent manner.

Assumptions:

- Open a small-business checking account linked to a money market account with $50,000. The account is FDIC insured up to $250,000.
- Use the indicated ratios for investment disbursement.
- $50,000 in a CD will earn ($50,000 x 1.25 percent) $624/year.
- $50,000 in a MMA will earn ($50,000 x 0.25 percent) $125/year.
- Tax liens earn from 6 percent to 25 percent interest per year. For illustration purposes, let's say 10 percent per year.
- Funds left in the money market account will earn 0.25 percent, the MMA interest. Being prudent, we have reserves.

The reserves will be used to purchase additional certificates and for family needs.

	Amounts	Ratio	Investment Earnings	CD Earning
Investment accounts:	$50,000.00	100%	$4,268.75	$624.00
Family reserve:	$5,000.00	10%	$12.50	
Tax lien reserve:*	$2,500.00	5%	$6.25	
Tax lien:	$42,500.00	85%	$4,250.00	

*This reserve is for the following year acquisitions.

As you can see from the above illustration, the investment account has conservatively earned $4,268.75, whereas the certificate of deposit has only earned $624.00. This is $3,644.75 more.

INCOME		
Tax liens:	$4,250.00	
Money market (reserves):	$18.75	
Outstanding loans:	$0.00	
Other:	$0.00	
Gross Scheduled Income =	$4,268.75	
EXPENSES		
Account maintenance:	$0.00	
Abstractor	$125.00	
Net Operating Income	$4,143.75	CFBT

Cash Flow: As discussed elsewhere, cash flow is of utmost importance.

Measurements:

Your initial cash investment (ICI) is $50,000.00.

Your Gross Scheduled Income (GOI) is $4,268.75.

Cash-on-Cash Return = CFBT/CI ($4,144.00/$50,000.00) = 8.29 percent.

SECTION 5   Cash Flow

5.0   Introduction

There are many ways to calculate your financial investment. The purpose of this book is to instruct you how to make your investments in a purely logical manner to maximize your cash flow.

5.1   Basic Calculations

Cash Flow	The asset's cash inflows less all of its cash outflows during a given period of time Cash Flow = Cash in − Cash Out
Cash Flow After Taxes (CFAT)	All cash inflows less all cash outflows during a given period of time, after taxes
Cash Flow Before Taxes (CFBT)	All cash inflows less all cash outflows during a given period of time, before taxes
Cash-on-Cash Return	The return on cash invested as a percentage over a year period
Cash Return on Investment	The amount of cash returned on an investment or the ratio of the remaining cash after debt service to invested capital Cash-on-Cash Return = Cash Flow Before Taxes/Cash Investment
Compound Interest	Computing interest where you apply the interest rate to the principal amount and to the accumulated interest $1,000 at 12% compounded interest per year Interest = Principal x Rate x Time Interest = $1,000 x 12% x 1 year

Raising the Family Without Taking a Hit

Initial Cash investment (ICI)	This is your initial investment
Money Management	The process of budgeting, spending, saving, and investing

SECTION 6   The Home Office

6.0   According to the IRS

Employees and self-employed individuals are permitted to deduct for a home office if the office is exclusively used on a regular basis under any of the following conditions:

A. The office is used by the taxpayer for administrative or management activities of the taxpayer's trade or business.

B. There is no other fixed location of the trade or business where the taxpayer conducts substantial administrative or management activities of the trade or business.

C. If a self-employed taxpayer maintains an office in the home, the expenses are deductible for AGI.

Deduction and limitations for the home office expenses are computed using the following two categories of expense:

A. Expenses directly related to the office

- Direct expenses include operating expenses that are used in the business as well as other expenses that relate solely to the office, such as painting and decorating just the office.

B. Expenses indirectly related to the office

- Indirect expenses are the prorated share (based on square foot) of expenses that benefit the entire house or apartment, such as mortgage interest (or rent), real estate taxes, insurance, utilities, and maintenance.

6.1 Home Setup

Designate a room in your home that you can use exclusively for work. The room should contain the following items at a minimum:

- A. four-drawer legal lateral file cabinet
- B. work desk
- C. computer and monitor
- D. color laser printer
- E. telephone

6.2 Internet

Secure a fast Internet connection from your local ISP. Once you have acquired it, connect a smart switch to it.

APPENDIX A

COMMONLY USED WORDS AND PHRASES

COMMONLY USED WORDS AND PHRASES

abatement—A reduction or decrease.

acceleration clause—A condition in a real estate financing instrument giving the lender the power to declare all sums owing the lender immediately due and payable upon the happening of an event such as sale of the property or a delinquency in the repayment of the note.

ad valorem—A Latin phrase meaning "according to value." An assessment of taxes against a property according to its value.

agent—One who acts for and with authority from another called the principal.

agreement—An exchange of promises, a mutual understanding or arrangement, or a contract. All agreements must be in writing and acknowledged by all parties.

appraisal—An opinion of value of property resulting from an analysis of facts about the property.

appraiser—An individual qualified by education, training, and experience who is hired to estimate the value of real property based on experience, judgment, facts, and use of formal appraisal processes.

appreciation—An increase in value of property due to changes in market conditions, inflation, or other causes.

assessor—A public official who establishes the value of property for taxation purposes.

borrowers—Individuals, revocable trusts, and LLCs.

executed contract—Contracts that are signed by all parties. Sometimes referred to as signed in counterpart.

fair market value—The highest price that a buyer willing but not compelled to buy would pay and the lowest a seller willing but not compelled to sell would accept.

full recourse—The borrowers must sign personally for the loan.

income—There are three types of income. **Earned or ordinary income**—derived from the hours you exchange at your job for financial compensation (wages or salaries). **Portfolio or tax-free**—interest income on bank deposits, dividends, or capital gains. This income group includes tax-free income (not an increase of wealth) such as municipal and state bonds. **Passive or capital gain**—capital gain results from the sale or exchange of assets used in a trade or business or held for investment. Passive income is derived from the ownership of rental property, author's royalties, and income generated from owning patents or license agreements.

nonrecourse debt—This type of financing does not require the borrower to assume personal liability for the loan. If the borrower defaults on the loan, the lender can take ownership of the property in a foreclosure proceeding, but the lender is limited only to the value of the collateral (property).

note—A legal document that obligates a borrower to repay a loan at a stated interest rate during a specified period of time.

operational expenses—The day-to-day operating expenses from running a property. These expenses typically include property taxes, insurance, maintenance, trash collection, utilities, and management fees. Other expenses may be marketing fees, postage, cell phones, employees, etc.

parcel number—Parcel number or assessor's parcel number is the unique method by which properties are identified, especially for tax purposes.

payback period—The period of time until you recover your initial cash investment (down payment).

real property—Land and appurtenances, including anything of a permanent nature such as structures, trees, minerals, and the interest, benefits, and inherent rights thereof.

redemption—After a period called the "redemption period" expires, investors, often for only the taxes, penalties, and interest due, can purchase the property.

APPENDIX B

TAX LIENS

TAX LIENS

State	Type	Bid Type/OTC	Interest Rate
Alabama	Lien	Premium/Yes	12% annum
Alaska	Deed	Varies/ Yes	N/A
Arizona	Lien	Bid down/Yes	16% annum
Arkansas	Deed	Premium/No	N/A
California	Deed	Premium/No	N/A
Colorado	Lien	Premium/Varies	Varies
Connecticut	Deed hybrid	Premium/No	18% annum
Delaware	Deed hybrid	Premium/No	15% penalty
Florida	Lien	Bid down/ No liens but deeds sold	18% down to 5% minimum
Georgia	Deed hybrid	Premium/No	20% penalty
Hawaii	Deed hybrid	Premium/No	12% annum
Idaho	Deed	Premium/No	N/A
Illinois	Lien	Bid down/No	18% penalty*
Indiana	Lien	Premium/No	10-15% penalty**
Iowa	Lien	Rotates/No	24% annum
Kansas	Deed	Premium/No	N/A
Kentucky	Lien	Premium/No	12% annum
Louisiana	Deed hybrid	Bid down/No	12% annum plus 5% penalty
Maine	Deed	Sealed/No	N/A
Maryland	Lien	Premium/Yes	6% to 24% annum
Massachusetts	Deed hybrid	Premium/No	16% annum
Michigan	Deed	Premium/No	N/A
Minnesota	Deed	Premium/Yes	N/A
Mississippi	Lien	Premium/Yes	18% annum on lien
Missouri	Lien	Premium/No	10% annum + 8% on further taxes
Montana	Lien	Rotates/Yes	10% annum + 2% penalty
Nebraska	Lien	Rotates/Yes	14% annum
Nevada	Deed	Premium/No	N/A

State	Type	Bidding/Premium	Interest/Penalty
New Hampshire	Deed	Premium/No	N/A
New Jersey	Lien	Bid Down on Premium/No	18% annum
New Mexico	Deed	Premium/No	N/A
New York	Deed	Premium/No	N/A
North Carolina	Deed	Premium/No	N/A
North Dakota	Lien	Premium/No	12% annum
Ohio	Deed & Lien	Premium/No	18% annum for lien
Oklahoma	Lien	Rotates/Yes	8% annum
Oregon	Deed	Premium/Varies	N/A
Pennsylvania	Deed hybrid varies by property	Premium/Varies	10% when applicable
Rhode Island	Deed hybrid	Premium/No	10% penalty plus 1% penalty a month starting with seventh month
South Carolina	Lien	Premium/Yes	8% to 12% annum
South Dakota	Lien	Premium/Yes	12% annum
Tennessee	Deed hybrid	Premium/No	10% annum
Texas	Deed hybrid	Premium/Varies	25% penalty
Utah	Deed	Premium/No	N/A
Vermont	Lien	Varies by town	12% annum
Virginia	Deed	Premium/No	N/A
Washington	Deed	Premium/No	N/A
West Virginia	Lien	Premium/No liens but deeds sold	12% annum
Wisconsin	Deed	Premium and sealed/No	N/A
Wyoming	Lien	Rotates/Yes	15% annum plus 3% penalty

APPENDIX C

REDEMPTION PERIODS

REDEMPTION PERIODS

State	Redemption Period
Alabama	Three years
Alaska	One year
Arizona	Three to five years
Arkansas	Thirty days
California	N/A
Colorado	Three years
Connecticut	One year
Delaware	Sixty days
Florida	Two years
Georgia	One year
Hawaii	One year
Idaho	N/A
Illinois	Two to three years
Indiana	One year
Iowa	Two years
Kansas	N/A
Kentucky	One year
Louisiana	Three years
Maine	N/A
Maryland	Six months
Massachusetts	Six months
Michigan	N/A
Minnesota	N/A
Mississippi	Two years
Missouri	Two years
Montana	Three years
Nebraska	Three years
Nevada	N/A
New Hampshire	N/A
New Jersey	Two years
New Mexico	N/A
New York	N/A
North Carolina	N/A
North Dakota	Three years
Ohio	Three years for lien

Raising the Family Without Taking a Hit

Oklahoma	Two years
Oregon	N/A
Pennsylvania	One year when applicable
Rhode Island	One year
South Carolina	One year
South Dakota	Three years
Tennessee	One year
Texas	Six months to two years
Utah	N/A
Vermont	One year
Virginia	N/A
Washington	N/A
West Virginia	Seventeen months
Wisconsin	N/A
Wyoming	Four years

APPENDIX D

ABSTRACTORS

Raising the Family Without Taking a Hit

ABSTRACTORS

Each company listed below offers different levels of service. Please review their offerings on their websites.

COMPANY	SERVING
Abstracts, Incorporated 585 Steward Avenue Garden City, NY 11530 (516) 683-1000 E-mail: info@AbstractsInc.com	Long Island, NY
Abstractor Services Inc. 3195 Dayton Xenia Road Suite 900-397 Beavercreek, OH 45434 (937) 675-2700 http://www.AbstractorServices.com	Ohio
American Document & Title LLC 1300 Whitacre Dive Clearwater, FL 33764 (727) 412-8010 http://www.AmeriDocsTitleSearch.com	Nationwide
ASK Land Title Services, LLC 38 Fieldstone Lane Candia, NH 03034 (603) 483-1039 http://www.AskTitleServices.com Email: Title.Orders@ASKTitleServices.com	Connecticut, Maine, New Hampshire, and Rhode Island
Easy Title Search 7950 S. Military Trail Suite 102 Lake Worth, FL 33463 (855) 888-4853	All of Florida, Georgia, Maryland, Ohio, and Massachusetts

http://www.EasyTitleSearch.com	Limited coverage in Alabama, Arizona, Illinois, Kentucky, Michigan, Missouri, Nevada, New Jersey, New Mexico, New York, Pennsylvania, and Washington
FastTitleSearch.com, LLC http://www.FastTitleSearch.com E-mail: support@FastTitleSearch.com	Florida
Florida Title Search http://www.FloridaTitleSearch.com	Florida
Nationwide Abstractor Services 2100 US-19 Alt. Palm Harbor, FL 34683 (800) 346-9152 http://www.NationwideTitleClearing.com	Nationwide
Oklahoma Abstractor's Directory http://www.ok.gov/abstractor/Abstractor_Directory	Oklahoma
Orange Abstractor Services 222 Greenwich Avenue Goshen, NY 10924 (845) 294-3331	New York State
Partners Abstract Corp. 1025 Old Country Road #409 Westbury, NY 11590 (516) 338-2655	Metro New York, Long Island, and mid-Hudson New York

E-mail: bobby@PartnersAbstract.com	
Pro Title USA Multiple offices across the United States Headquarters: Holland, PA (888) 878-8081 http://www.ProTitleUSA.com E-mail: info@ProTitleUSA.com	Nationwide
REO America Abstract Inc. 123 S. Broad Street Suite 1225 Philadelphia, PA 19109 (215) 320-5770 http://www.REOAmericaAbstract.com	Delaware, Maryland, New Jersey, New York, Pennsylvania, and Washington, DC
Title Searcher (866) 604-3674 http://www.TitleSearcher.com	Arkansas, Kentucky, North Carolina, South Carolina, Tennessee, and Virginia
US Title Records 160 Greentree Drive Suite 101 Dover, DE 19904 Fax: (302) 269-3942 http://www.USTitleRecords.com E-mail: Office@USTitleRecords.com	Nationwide
Vital Abstract LLC 3700 Route 27 Suite 102B Princeton, NJ 08540 (732) 230-2574 http://www.VitalAbstract.com E-mail: sales@VitalAbstract.com	New Jersey

APPENDIX E

ONLINE TAX LIEN AUCTION HOUSES

ONLINE TAX LIEN AUCTION HOUSES

Bid4Assets (877) 427-7387 http://www.Bid4Assets.com
BidMaricopa.com Charles "Hos" Hoskins, Treasurer Maricopa County, AZ 301 W. Jefferson Avenue Suite 100 Phoenix, AZ 85003 (602) 506-8511 http://www.BidMaricopa.com
Civic Source (888) 387-8033 http://www.civicsource.com E-mail: support@CivicSource.com
Grant Street Group 339 Sixth Street Suite 1400 Pittsburg, PA 15222 (412) 391-5555 http://www.grantstreet.com/auctions/tax_lien_certificate_auctions/
Realauction.com, LLC Plantation, FL 33324 Phone: (954) 734-7400 Fax: (954) 424-7601 http://www.RealAuction.com E-mail: customerservice@RealAuction.com

www.ingramcontent.com/pod-product-compliance
Lightning Source LLC
Chambersburg PA
CBHW070335190526
45169CB00005B/1908